ST MINVER
Its Bays and Byways

Including Rock, Porthilly, Trebetherick and Polzeath with Port Quin

The author at Padstow; Bray Hill and Daymer Bay in the
background

Rock beach

ST MINVER, ITS BAYS AND BYWAYS

including

ROCK
PORTHILLY
TREBETHERICK
POLZEATH

with

PORT QUIN

Jack Ingrey

TABB HOUSE

First published 1994
Tabb House, 7 Church Street, Padstow, Cornwall PL28 8BG

A catalogue record of this title is available from the British Library

ISBN 1 873951 07 8

Printed by Short Run Press Ltd, Exeter, Devon

CONTENTS

ACKNOWLEDGEMENTS

My acknowledgments and grateful thanks to Mr R. Tellam Hocking of Trebetherick for the loan and use of his numerous Scrap Books of St Minver Parish, and to Malcolm McCarthey of Padstow for the use of photographs from his collection of old Cornish photographs.

Jack Ingrey, March 1994

Malcolm McCarthey's photographs appear on pp. 15, 17 (two), 21, 22 (two), 25, 29, 35, 44, 51 (two), 55 and 69; there are also photographs by Steven Cull on pp. 61 and 62 and on the back cover (three) and by Ray Bishop on pp. 15, 55 and the front cover.

Other photographs are by the Author.

LIST OF ILLUSTRATIONS

FOREWORD

St MINVER parish is situated on the north coast of Cornwall, bounded seawards by the Bristol Channel; on the east by the parishes of St Endellion and St Kew, and on the south and west by the river Camel. Wadebridge is four and a half miles away from the south-east boundary, and Padstow about half a mile by ferry on the opposite side of the Camel estuary.

The estuary and seaward boundaries embrace the unspoiled beaches of Porthilly and Rock, Daymer, Polzeath, Lundy and Epphaven – the latter two being approachable only by foot-path. Rock-bound Port Quin on the northern fringe of the parish is partly within the parish of St Endellion.

St Minver parish, which covers about 5,300 acres, is divided into the Highlands and the Lowlands; it contains three churches, a holy well and a world-famous golf course.

The main communities are Rock, Porthilly, Stoptide, Penmayne, Splatt, Pityme and Tredrissick, Trebetherick, New and Old Polzeath.

About twenty farms are scattered throughout this large parish, several of which have been occupied by the same families for generations.

The main crops are wheat, barley and roots, together with cattle rearing. In recent years several caravan parks have been developed on their acres.

St Minver has roots going back into the Iron Age on Pentire Point where the ramparts and defences of the Rumps cliff castle are clearly visible.

The parish is sparsely wooded and trees grow high only in valleys. There is little of architectural interest except the churches, the Rock Sailing Club building and the Folly – Doyden Castle, made famous in the Poldark TV series. But the fascination lies on the shores of the estuary which has brought countless visitors and immigrants to savour the boating, seaside golf, windsurfing, water skiing, and at Polzeath the flat, golden sands for children, and safe bathing.

Coming to St Minver, like coming to several other Cornish parishes, does mean an adjustment to the rural way of life. The main roads are narrow, with many bends, and the lanes leading from them are narrower still, often flanked by high stone hedges, bushes and deep ditches. In summer they are flower filled and to drive fast through them is foolish because their beauty is missed, and above all, dangerous, both to drivers and unfortunate pedestrians.

When walking on public footpaths through fields, fasten all gates, for wandering cattle can cause serious accidents. Keep to the paths, and if there is an obstruction, walk around it, and should there be difficulty in determining the position of the path, walk around the edge of the field and cause as little damage as possible to crops. Always keep your dog under proper control for if it is unaccustomed to open country and cattle it can easily become excited and unwittingly worry sheep, or cause cows to panic and even to rush blindly over cliff tops to their deaths.

Tread warily on the estuary and dunes; tramping feet denudes them of their marram grass covering, and when this happens, later winter gales blow away the exposed root networks and the dunes recede. In several parts of Cornwall this has happened, and consequently dune areas have been closed off for long periods and extensive and costly replanting has had to be carried out.

During hot summers, dunes, cornfields and headlands become tinder dry, and the careless dropping of lighted matches and cigarette ends has in the past caused many expensive fires and the disruption of farm and wildlife. Discarded jars and bottles can also catch the sun's rays and cause fires. This, and other litter, particularly plastic articles, can when eaten kill unsuspecting cattle.

North Cornwall has a bounty of wild flowers, many of which are rarities, and each year the list grows longer as some common varieties become scarcer. They depend on us for their survival, so whether we are residents – local or immigrant – or holidaymakers, let us admire, tread softly and warily, and not be tempted to pick them.

By observing these few countryside rules the magic of St Minver can be preserved, whether it be at the windswept summit of Pentire, the rock pools of Greenaway, the spongy fairways of the golf course, the sheltered lanes around Porthilly, the footpaths which intersect the Highland and the Lowland fields, or the still unfrequented places known only to parishioners and those who cherish these acres.

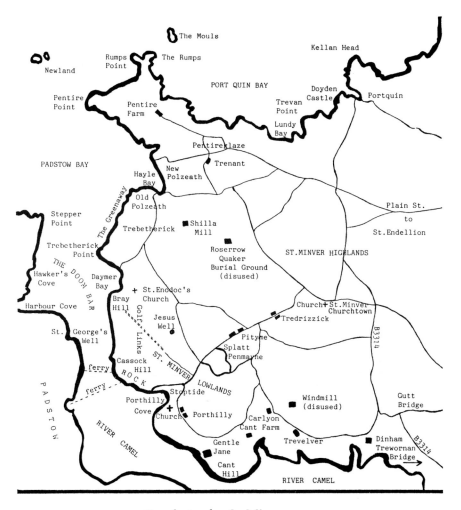

Roads in the St Minver area

TREWORNAN BRIDGE TO PORTHILLY VIA DINHAM AND PORTHILLY TO ROCK

Trewornan Bridge to Porthilly

TREWORNAN BRIDGE is about 150 years old and straddles the boundaries of St Minver and Egloshayle parishes. It has all the appearance of a medieval bridge with its four pointed arches with spans of seventeen to twenty-one feet and handsome piers.

Legend rides across the bridge in the shape of a phantom coach. In the early hours one morning in the early nineteenth century, two washerwomen sisters named Rosie and Honor Eley left their home near St Minver parish church and went in their pony trap to do a day's washing at Trewornan Manor, up a driveway a short distance from the bridge, on the St Minver side. Arriving at their destination at about five o'clock, they were standing by the closed entrance gate to the drive when they saw a coach and four approaching. As it crossed the bridge they heard the postilions shout "Gate! Gate!" The women rushed to open the heavy gates and, as the coach swept through, one of them shouted "What time of day is it please?" From within the coach came a man's gruff voice: "Time for

1

1.   Trewornan Bridge

the dead to be walking and the living to be sleeping." The astonished women followed the coach up the drive, but when they reached the Manor they found the house in darkness and no sign of the coach. The sisters told the story to their friends in the village and stood by it to their dying days. One wonders, though, if they looked around the back of the house, if they mentioned their experience to their employers, and if a number of people kept silent about another load of smuggled goods that had almost reached its destination.

Let us pause for a moment on the bridge and look eastwards across the water meadows to Chapel Amble. Amble means 'on the estuary', and the River Amble joins the Camel river at Trewornan. Between the village and Trewornan Bridge is the important Walmsley Sanctuary, owned and managed by the Cornwall Bird Watching and Preservation Society. Here forty acres of marshland have been contoured into grassland

and freshwater pools for feeding migratory birds. This is private land, and members of the Society can only go there with special authority. Turning westwards now, below Trewornan Bridge at Burniere Point you will see a well-constructed hide where members can watch the activities of winter migrants including white fronted geese, and all year round resident swans.

Here also is a dyke built across the marshes to prevent high tide flooding which, coupled with heavy rain, often used to cause extensive flooding across the road at Chapel Amble.

At one time barges from Padstow and Wadebridge could be rowed at high tide under Trewornan Bridge up to Penpont Bridge in Chapel Amble village. Among the cargoes of sand, coal and seaweed, a keg of spirits or a box of tea was sometimes concealed, for the village was reasonably free from Revenue patrolmen. Until 1920 this free flow of river traffic continued, the barges loading back with grain, but with the building of the dyke navigation came to an end. During free-trading and smuggling days a receiving and distribution point was identified by inserting the bottom end of a bottle into the external wall of a roadside building and at Lands Farm the old cider press building is said to have such a bottle still in existence.

The road from Trewornan Bridge to Rock is busy at all times but pedestrians can walk via Gutt Bridge to Pityme, where one takes the second turning on the left, and for St Minver Churchtown the third turning on the left.

But having reached Gutt Bridge and ascended the hill, there is a pleasant and quieter road leading to Porthilly and Rock from the first left-hand fork leading down to Dinham, where there was once a salt water tide mill. We pass caravan parks at Dinham Farm and Little Dinham, and from the valley the narrow road rises through high hedges to Trevelver Farm where there are fine views of the estuary, with the derelict Camel Quarries rising from the water's edge.

Between Trevelver and Carlyon Farms stands the shell of an old windmill in a field on the right hand side of the road.

Windmills are nearly always found in parishes which border the edges of tidal estuaries, and St Minver had at least five. Three windmills were located at Roserrow Farm where each mill had a field named after it – Little, Western and Great Windmill fields. There was another mill on the tenement of Moyles Keiro, but none of these have survived except the prominent ruin standing on the top of Carlyon Hill. This can be seen as a landmark from the sea, St Breoke Downs and St Issey, but as one passes along the road by Trevelver Farm it is not visible from road level. The ruined tower has walls about three feet thick, is thirty feet high and flat topped. Traces of white plastering can still be seen on the external walls, which must have enhanced its value as a landmark. St Minver, like St Issey, was one of the finest corn-growing parishes in Cornwall.

From Carlyon Farm the right hand fork of the road leads to Higher Penmayne and Pityme, but we take the left fork which leads to Porthilly, passing a lane on the left that leads down to what was once the derelict Cant Farm. Now the farmhouse and outbuildings have been restored into a hamlet of seven all year round luxury holiday dwellings.

As the road swings round in a wide curve a left-hand turning leads down to Gentle Jane, the lovely name for an unspoiled cove. Who this mythical lady was, no one knows. Perhaps she once lived here alone with only birds and wild animals for company. Perhaps her name was a cover-up, and she had a hand in local smuggling and under-cover activities. She may have even emigrated to St Merryn, for on the Harlyn road there is an old cottage with the same name. Or it could be the corruption of a forgotten Cornish phrase.

Cant Hill is lovely at all seasons, its contours best seen from the Padstow side of the estuary. The word Cant derives from the Latin *canti*, meaning corner. When the Romans occupied Britain they looked upon the extreme south-east of the country as a corner, and it became Canti, and later Kent. St Minver parish, which lies between the Bristol Channel and the Camel estuary, juts out in a similar manner as the county of Kent.

The whole of the parish can be termed as a *canti* and its occupants *cantii* – dwellers of the corner; and Cant Hill – the hill on the corner.

We have recently passed Carlyon Farm which, in 1289 was spelt Carleghion (Car = camp or fort; Leghion = Roman Legion). A Roman Legion consisted of from 3,000 to 6,000 men, and there was a Roman fort at Nanstallon near Bodmin around AD 55-80. A detachment of soldiers could well have been stationed at Carlyon, and in their language would have called the region *canti* – a corner. Their purpose would have been to protect the estuary area from periodic raids by the Irish.

It was from the word *canti* that the well-known Cornish surname of Kent originated, having become established by 1327. Between 1700 and 1750 the Kents comprised over four per cent of the population of St Minver parish. In the second half of the eighteenth century they were reduced to just one and a half per cent, and by the mid-twentieth century only four adult Kents remained in the parish. The cause of the decline was due to a migration to the clay areas of St Austell.

Our walk now takes us down to Porthilly Cove where one can either return to Stoptide, Splatt and Pityme, or proceed along the beach to Rock.

Porthilly to Rock

PORTHILLY fringes a small cove to the right of Rock and Stoptide. It is possible that its origins were of a monastic order and that the two farmhouses near the church were the House of Labour and the House of Rest, belonging to Bodmin Priory. By 1284 the two farms Porthilly Grey and Porthilly Eglos were in church hands and remain so today.

In 1720 historian John Norden wrote 'Perdille [Porthilly] a hamlet and harbor wherin of late yeares ther were few or noe

2. Looking towards Cant Hill beyond the Rock Sailing Club building and Porthilly

houses, now by their industrious fishinge and the blessing of God, the inhabitantes so increase in abilitye as their prosperitye allureth others to resorte to the place and dailie increase the buyldinges, that in few yeares, if they contynue prayerfull and religious, it will grow to a pretie town'. How fortuitously he predicted the future of Porthilly and Rock, for although not having reached town status, thanks to the fashions in holidays their combined areas have greatly developed in our present century.

The narrow winding lane continues on past the farms towards Cant and West Park, with a left fork turning back to

3. Porthilly Farm

4. Porthilly Church

Pityme and a right fork leading to Carlyon, Trevelver, Tregenna and Dinham, where it joins the main road from Wadebridge to Rock and Polzeath.

For the moment, though, we turn right at Porthilly Farm and proceed along the path to the lychgate leading to Porthilly Church where this small building, dedicated to St Michael, sits almost on the shore. The churchyard walls are lapped by the surging tides which sweep up the Camel estuary. It was once known as the South Chapel, its sister being St Enodoc or North Chapel, with St Menefreda as their mother church.

Porthilly Church is of Norman origin, and as we enter we can see traces of work of that period in the nave, chancel and south transept. In the thirteenth century the transept was widened and a lancet window formed in the east wall, together with a piscina to serve the chapel.

Further alterations were made in the fifteenth century when the south wall of the chancel was taken down and a chancel aisle added. Two arches were then formed – one to support the roof above the south chancel, and the other in the east wall of the transept to give access to the newly built chapel.

In 1865 St Michael's was 'restored' by the architect J.P. St Aubyn, and here again he applied the same ruthlessness as he had to St Minver church and many others by pulling out stonework, timbering and pavings; plastering over lovely stonework to walls and laying ugly Victorian chequerboard floorings. The lower part of the chancel screen still remains, and it is possible that the pulpit was fashioned from part of the upper structure. A newel staircase gave access to the top of the screen and was built into the north wall of the chancel, and part of it still exists.

Happily the porch and vestry, although modern, harmonize well with the older stonework. The Norman font is similar to the font in St Enodoc church.

A well-preserved slate memorial slab to William Rouncevall is attached to the wall behind the font and is worth a close inspection. The inscription around the perimeter reads 'Here lyeth the body of William Rounsevall who was buried the 25th

December Anno Dom 1659, Jane his wife was Buried ye 4th
of Aug's't 1679.'

Within the rectangle are four beautifully carved formal
roses, one in each corner, and in the centre is the epitaph
which reads:

> Death's but a Sleepe & if a Sleepe Why then
> To Bed the Grave dothe soe much Trouble man
> How Welcome's death to faith though sprung from Vice.
> Raising us to Ceelestial Paradise.
> The Peenitent by faith doe truly prove
> The Ocean Mercie of the God of Love.
> Then Dye to Live & gaine that highly priz'd
> Elected soules shall be Imortaliz'd.

Near the Rouncevall memorial is a notice about Helen
Proffit's Legacy which states that this lady in her Will left five
pounds a year to be paid out of her Estate in Porthilly for the
remainder of a term of 1,000 years to William Kent of Trefresa,
his heirs and Executors in Trust for the use of the poor of the
Lowland of St Minver who did not receive weekly pay.

Near the church door is a fine four-holed granite cross that
once stood at the west end of the chapel. The shaft is missing,
and a theory has been put forward that it might match the
shaft of a cross just inside the eastern entrance to Padstow
churchyard. These holed crosses are fairly rare and probably
originated during the fifth and eighth centuries when they
marked the sites of preaching stations, boundaries and guide-
posts to the church.

In the churchyard are many interesting slate memorials with
incised epitaphs, and among them is this delicate message from
Elizabeth Cann and her son Thomas Vinton Cann:

> Gently, softly, lightly tread
> In the region of the dead.
> Here and there behold a friend.
> Reader, see thy latter end.

5. Rock from Porthilly Churchyard

For sheer pomposity the following must be a winner:

Embossed in the dust below are the precious remains
of Phillipa Eales daughter of Richard and Anne Hawkey
of Trefresa in this parish when cruel death suddenly
wrenched from the arms of her affectionate parents to
harmonize with the Seraphic Choir May 7 1813 aged 5 years
Farewell thou dearest of my heart
Which neither tears nor prayers can save.
Tis Death's redoubled pain to part
And leave such beauty in the grave
Till the last hour of general doom
Kind angels guard this precious trust.
Watch the cold embers of her tomb
And timely wake her slumbering dust.

As we stand in this sea-lapped churchyard looking across
at Padstow town, let us turn back the clock to the nineteenth

century and visualise a host of sailing vessels crowded in and around the harbour. From them come small rowing boats, each with a consignment of men, women and children, all of them emigrants about to set sail to the furthest parts of the earth, but before leaving they anchor beneath these grey churchyard walls and pass silently up the steps and into the church to pray for a safe journey and a successful life in their new surroundings.

From the north-east side of the churchyard we descend those steps as did the emigrants, and enter Porthilly Cove where we cross the saltings to Rock. Porthilly Cove is shallow and rather muddy. At neap tides dinghies can sail on the river all day, although low tide exposes numerous sand bars. At spring tides the river dries out too completely for any dighy sailing at low water.

The saltings flora include common scurvy grass, sea spurry, sea plantain, sea purslane, glasswort, seabit, sea beet, thrift, scentless mayweed, yarrow and many more varieties of estuary plants.

At low tide the sand banks are of outstanding interest for bird watchers and nature photographers. In autumn and winter under the shelter of the cliffs below Rock and armed with binoculars and cameras with telephoto lenses, they can observe resident and migrant wintering wildfowl and rarities on most days. Among the many species seen are:

> Black throated and great northern divers
> Cormorant, shag
> Ducks: mallard, shelduck, teal, widgeon
> Curlew, dunlin, greenshank, redshank, knot
> Sanderling, turnstone, snipe, whimbrel
> Gulls: common, greater and lesser
> black-backed, black headed, herring, kittiwake
> Grey heron
> Lapwing, ringed plover
> Oystercatcher
> Raven, rook, jackdaw

6. Porthilly saltings

7. Rock and Porthilly Bay from Chapel Stile, Padstow

Mute swan
Little grebe

As we leave Porthilly Cove and saltings, the foreshore is now sandy. Note the unusual vertical stonework to the sea wall of several of the cliff-edge properties. Ahead is the dominant bulk of the Rock Sailing Club, once an old grain warehouse doomed for demolition, but in 1976 saved and transformed internally, and renovated externally without losing its original character. Until 1991, across the estuary on Padstow's north quay until 1991 stood a similar store known as the Red Brick Building. After much local deliberation it was demolished and a similar building was built. Unfortunately, it is insensitive to the Padstow vernacular, lacking a Delabole slate roof and having the addition of pretentious granite columns. Its top floors are used for flats and the ground floor houses the Padstow gigs and the Tourist Office.

A few yards from the sailing club is the stone slipway which leads us up to Rock village, joining the road from Pityme over which we have previously walked.

Rock

ROCK looks out over a broad lagoon formed in the Camel estuary when the tide is full, and is sheltered from Atlantic swells by a sand bar at the mouth. The main channel of the Camel comes in close to the shore, carrying currents up to six knots that run near the boat moorings. Long stretches of golden sand backed by marram-clad dunes and rocky cliffs border this lagoon from Rock to Daymer Bay and the open sea beyond. This natural asset has made the small village one of the most sought-after places for residence and holidays in Cornwall, for here all varieties of water sport, skiing, canoeing, wind surfing and sailing can be practiced by the initiated or taught by competent instructors.

Rock was once a riverside hamlet linked to Padstow by Black Rock Ferry, and Black Rock (or Black Tor) gave its name to the hamlet. Composed of greenstone, it was the only outcrop visible amid the surrounding waves and sand dunes. Today, even at low tide, hardly a rock can be seen.

In 1337 the ferry was held in common by the tenants of the Manor of Penmayne. In 1469 John Bussell and John Rawlyn, freemen, took the ferry rights at the annual rental of eight shillings and contracted that the passage boat should be well and sufficiently kept in repair, and that if the boat afterwards chanced to be broken, they would new-build the said boat. In 1820 the ferry was much improved by the then proprietor who erected on the rock in the middle of the sands, where a signal was made for the boat, a house and a stable for the accommodation of passengers and their horses. Before, passengers crossing by the ferry were obliged to wait exposed to the vagaries of the elements. There were fatalities on this narrow stretch of water, for on October 13th, 1836 John Cock, aged thirty of Black Rock, was drowned, and on December 9th, 1894 the ferry sank and two men were drowned. The ferry is now operated by the Padstow Harbour Commissioners who use large motor launches. Departure points are from Rock beach, and further down at low water, and there is nowhere to wait out of the rain.

Rock has no distinct centre. Its shops are scattered; there is no school and no church, although there is a Methodist chapel.

During the 1930s considerable individual development took place along the waterfront, and by the early 1950s there were signs of over-development after a major sewage scheme was completed and many planning applications vn were approved. Rock was fast becoming an area of second or holiday homes, with land values inflating yearly and properties changing hands at sky-high prices. This rise greatly hindered local residents in rented properties from buying their homes, for their incomes could not match those of the ever-increasing flow of immigrants. The increased popularity of Rock is such that in July 1978 the *Cornish Guardian* reported that the Chief Planning

8. The Rock to Padstow ferry in about the 1950s

9. The ferry in the 1990s

Officer said that some home owners in St Minver parish were claiming that their property was in Rock because it sounded more exclusive and added value to their property.

Many local people have moved out since Rock was 'discovered' and a great deal of outside money was poured in too quickly, to an area that was not geared for rapid expansion, and it is still struggling from these effects. Perhaps the planning authorities were to blame; and one cannot really blame those local people who could do so, for selling out at high prices to speculators and affluent immigrants for their sailing and golfing holidays.

During the 1920s the Rock Sailing Club was formed by Rear-Admiral Hext Rogers, and the golf course spread its fairways from this small village away to St Enodoc. Rock Villas council houses, also built during the 1920s, were probably the most exclusive and expensively-sited local authority owned houses in the county, based on current values. They have now been demolished and replaced by bungalows for the elderly. The Rock Hotel was also built with an eye to the increasing sailing coterie. It was demolished in 1976, rebuilt and renamed The Mariners Inn in memory of the first inn of that name. In the *Sherborne Mercury and Weekly Advertiser* of May 1769 we read that 'the ferry house was called the Rock Inn and Mariners Inn' and was described as 'a very commodious and ancient place for business where Thomas Chilcott keeps the public business and merchandise shop in the same house'.

Rock foreshore is delightful for family picnics. At low tide scores of small sailing craft are laid up along the beach and the continual slap of rope against metal mast can be music or otherwise to the ears of sunbathers. The slap of rope against wooden masts used to be an altogether more melodious sound.

Erosion has caused much shifting of sand below the foreshore roadway and railway sleepers have been placed against the dunes to prevent further invasion. The road ends at the old quarry, which is now cleared and levelled into a sheltered car park with a toilet block.

Published by J. E. OATEY, Wadebridge.   Rock Village.

10.   Rock Village and Rock Hotel in the early 1900s

Rock Village, Padstow.

11.   Rock Village from Porthilly Cove in the 1900s

12.   Rock foreshore

Along this road, opposite the ferry landing, is the Upper Deck Club and the Last Resort licensed restaurant. Scenes for the film *The Eagle has Landed* were shot along this area of shore.

The road verge and dunes are a yellow blaze of tall evening primrose plants in summer, and in winter north-west Atlantic gales bring stinging clouds of blown sand into the faces of those hardy walkers who venture along this stretch of the estuary. But whatever the season or time of day or state of the tide, the view of the estuary from Rock is unforgettable. See it at sunrise and high tide with the summer boats sleeping on the water; hear the sounds of waking gulls and Padstow; see the needle obelisk on Dinas Hill looking down at the old iron bridge and the narrowing estuary dominated by Cant Hill on the left with the desolate Camel Quarry on the right; see it through the eyes of John Betjeman:

When low tides drain the estuary gold
Small intersecting breakers far away
Ripple about a bar of shifting sand
Where centuries ago were waving woods . . .

From the slipway we complete our walk, passing Rock
Terrace, The Mariners on our left and Penmayne Flats on our
right. Short lanes on the left lead to St Enodoc Hotel and
Leisure Club, residential properties, and St Enodoc golf
club-house and golf course.

ST ENODOC

St Enodoc Golf Club

ST ENODOC Golf Club came into being in 1891 when a first general meeting was held in a quarry behind what is now St Enodoc Hotel, and some twenty participants paid their first annual membership subscriptions of five shillings, which was later raised to ten shillings.

The land was leased in 1900 from Dr Theophilus Hoskin who, on his death, was buried in St Enodoc churchyard. Mrs Hoskin straight away forbade any Sunday golf on the fairways around the church, removing the flags and reducing the course to twelve holes on that day.

A full eighteen-hole course was laid out by James Baird of Walton Heath in 1907, and again altered in the early 1920s. In 1949 the owner of the land decided to sell the course, together with Bray House. Backed by the Duchy of Cornwall, the course was purchased and a lease granted to the club as tenants under the secretaryship of Sir Clive Burn.

Many famous people have visited this 6,000 yard championship-standard course, among them, in 1921, Edward Prince of Wales, who became President in 1928 and continued

13.   The Prince of Wales playing golf at St Enodoc, about 1930

until he became uncrowned King upon the death of his father King George V. A.J. Balfour played on the course before he became Prime Minister, and in July 1950 King George VI, Queen Elizabeth (now the Queen Mother) and Princess Elizabeth were entertained to tea by the Captain and Committee. During World War II the young Duke of Kent, Princess Alexandra and Prince Michael stayed at St Enodoc Hotel and spent a lot of time in the club-house and Secretary's office where the Secretary, no doubt, had his hands full when instructed to entertain his young guests.

Sir John Betjeman called the golf course 'a lark haunted links . . . a course for Princes and Poets', and he saw 'a foursome puffing past the sunlit hedge . . . and all the singing grass busy with crickets and blue butterflies'. This marvellous par-69 course has many surprises for the unwary; the 6th hole which lies behind the enormous Himalaya bunker, reputedly the largest in the world, where your drive if not played short lands you inside its sandy mouth, forcing you to play

14.   The Himalaya bunker, about 1930

15.   The old club-house

backwards or give up. The 10th hole is also formidable where you take a line from the tee on the spire of St Enodoc church – crooked for many years but recently straightened.

The white-painted stones set along the path by the golf course were put there by Mr E.A.R. Burden, an honoured and popular secretary to the club; they are known as the Burden Stones.

A new club-house was opened by Sir Cecil Carr in 1937 and many further improvements to course and club have been carried out during the post-war years. A short 9-hole course was in being for many years and has latterly been extended into a full 18-hole course, named the Holywell Course with a length of 4,165 yards, ideal for holidaying golfers and residents who prefer a less strenuous and challenging round than that provided by its famous big brother, now known as the Church Course.

Rock to Daymer Bay via Bray Hill and St Enodoc Church

FROM the car park we follow the Coastal Path along the edge of the marram-clad sand dunes, passing the small hump of Cassock Hill with the green undulations, ridges and valleys of St Enodoc Golf Club fairways and greens on our right.

The dunes and golf course contain a varied collection of spring and summer flowers equal to any others from the coastal fringes of Cornwall. As we walk, some of the following flowers may be seen dependent upon the time of the year:

SPRING: Blackthorn, sea buckthorn, buttercup, bluebell, common storksbill, sea campion, gorse, primrose, thrift, dog violet

SUMMER: Kidney vetch, birdsfoot trefoil, mullein, tree mallow, red campion, ox-eye daisy, dodder, foxglove, ragwort, wild carrot.

Bray House stands amid a cluster of trees in the shadow of Bray Hill, and the 9th green and 10th tee are nearby. A diversion can be made at the green where the path leads on to a footbridge over a marsh, making a short cut to St Enodoc Church and the unfenced road leading back to Stoptide. But we follow the path past Bray House and reach the foot of Bray Hill. Here we have a choice: (a) follow the path to the left into Daymer Bay; (b) take the right-hand path past disused quarries and across the fairway to St Enodoc church; (c) ignore the paths and, if you are sound in wind and limb, climb up to the summit of Bray Hill where the panoramic view is spectacular.

Bray Hill (some maps spell it Brae, but Betjeman preferred Bray) is 200 feet high. Richard Thomas, aged 50, a retired mariner from Devon, built a house on .the south side on the site of a large rabbit warren. When its foundations were being excavated Saxon graves were uncovered, which contained skeletal remains laid out on rough slate slabs without encasing sides or tops. Thomas also acquired and kept in his house a bronze funerary urn with zig-zag decorations, which was found in the tumulus at the top of the hill.

An old Roman road from St Endellion passed through Plain Street and branched off at Pentire, while the main track continued to Moyles and Treglines, crossed the stream at Roserrow and continued in a straight line to Trebetherick. The road can be traced on the crest of the hill north of Trenain Farm, but from then on it has disappeared.

There appears to have been a Roman out-station on the landward side of Bray Hill on high ground near Trenain. Coins of the reign of the Emperor Gallienus (AD 260-268) have been found here, and no doubt the whole area around Bray Hill, St Enodoc and the Golf Course covers many archaeological secrets.

From the summit of Bray Hill we look back over the wide Camel estuary into Padstow, and up the river to the Iron Bridge and Dinas Hill and away to St Issey parish. Looking towards the estuary mouth, we see Stepper Point on our left

16. Trebetherick Point before the Second World War

17. St Enodoc Church from Bray Hill

and Pentire Point on our right, the rocky foreshore of Greenaway and the scattered houses of Trebetherick above, below us the tawny-gold sands of Daymer Bay, and as we look eastwards the fields and farms of the Highlands and Lowlands districts of this parish. Directly below and near the 10th green is St Enodoc church.

We make our way down to the foot of the hill, skirting the Green to the church.

St Enodoc Church

EVERYONE who has read the late Sir John Betjeman's poems will be familiar with this tiny church, crouching low in its graveyard surrounded by a stone hedge, which is surmounted by windswept tamarisks.

It is in the churchyard just beyond the lychgate, on the right-hand side, that our well-beloved Poet Laureate was laid to rest beside his mother on Tuesday May 22nd, 1984, amid pouring rain and the rumble of thunder. The interior of the church glowed with the wild flowers he loved, and at the private funeral were many parishioners whom he knew so well during his long association with St Minver parish. His bearers were his son, Paul Betjeman, son-in-law Rupert Lycett-Green, Christopher and Benjamin Barbour, Lord Eliot and Jonathan Stendall. On June 29th, 1984 a farewell service of thanksgiving for his life was held in Westminster Abbey, led by the Dean of Westminster. 2,000 people attended, from HRH Prince Charles to the Paddlestream Preservation Society, and members of the Royal Family including the Queen and the Queen Mother were represented. John Oakley read the poem 'Trebetherick', and music, church bells, poetry and silence – the poet's favourite sounds – were the theme. In Cornwall another service of thanksgiving was held in St Endellion church – also one of his favourites in which he worshipped during his later years.

18. Sir John
Betjman's grave

A semi-circular-headed Delabole slate headstone, with incised lettering 'John Betjeman 1906-1984' within a floral motif,
marks his grave less than half a mile from Treen, his Cornish
cottage near Daymer Lane. His poetic genius gave a bright
sheen of romance and nostalgia to ordinary people and
commonplace things, from lamp posts to railways, typists to
tidelines. He possessed that magic of insight which combined
humour and humility into something that really mattered. And
so he rests in the soil he loved where there is, in his own
words,

Lark song and sea sounds in the air
And splendour, splendour everywhere.

To return to St Enodoc church: why was it sited in such a
deserted landscape? Perhaps it was not, for a Cornish tradition
states that wherever there is a church with a spire, there is the
site of a pagan burial ground. Excavated human remains,
pottery and coins indicate that there was an ancient trading
post or hamlet in the vicinity. It was probably evacuated
because of violent sand storms, and now lies buried beneath
the green-clad dunes.

St Enodoc has had several names over the centuries. In 1434
it was known as St Guindoc; in 1603 Gwenedowe, Gwethenoc
or Kennet; on a 1620 map it was marked as St Edith; and in
the nineteenth century Nedye, Edye and Sinkininny.

The foundations of the church are hewn out of solid rock
and for some years, until the church was restored, a small
spring oozed from them. The structure is cruciform in origin,
and to it was added the low two-stage tower, which is
surmounted by a stumpy broach spire with a small trefoil-
headed window in each face of the broach. Over the centuries
wind and heat twisted the spire but recently it has been
straightened.

During the fifteenth century a south aisle was added. By the
nineteenth century the church was almost engulfed by sand
and the local population dubbed it 'sinking neddy' under the
impression that the building was sinking in the sand. The roof
became unsound, sand drifted in and the only access was
through a hole in the roof. A letter written from Padstow on
November 18th, 1859 by H.B. Thorp recalls a visit to the
church. 'It is half buried in the sand, so much so that I could
walk from the ground onto the roof. They have dug a path
down to the doorway and a service is performed there every
other fortnight'. By 1860 it was quite roofless, but in 1864 a
restoration took place under the supervision of the Reverend
Hart Smith, the work being carried out by local craftsmen.
There was evidently much to do, for a letter written by the

19. St Enodoc Church, from an old engraving

vicar's son stated that 'the sands had blown higher than the eastern gable; the wet came in freely; the high pews were mouldy-green and worm eaten, and bats flew about, living in the belfry'.

The communion table had two short legs because they rested on rock protruding from the foot of the east wall. This, however, was cut away and the legs made good. Everything of value was saved and reused wherever possible, and not needlessly destroyed. The total cost of the operation was £650 and included rebuilding some of the walls on proper foundations, renewing the roof, building the wall around the churchyard, and general tidying up. Much of these renovations were paid for by Mrs and Miss Sandys of St Minver House. They are commemorated in the porch and in the east window.

A further restoration took place in 1873 by the architect J.P. St Aubyn when he was engaged in restoring the mother church of St Minver, but mercifully, owing to the previous work, he was unable to pursue his usual stripping and gutting techniques.

20.   St Enodoc's interior in the 1990s

As we enter this lovely little building with its humble and west-country look, pale-green paned windows, slate floor, rounded wood roof, Norman arch and font with cable mouldings, it is plain to see the detail the poet used to bring it into national focus in his poem 'Sunday Afternoon Service in St Enodoc Church, Cornwall':

> My eyes, recovering in the sudden shade,
> Discern the long-known little things within –
> A map of France in damp above my pew,
> Grey-blue of granite in the small arcade . . .

On the south wall of the nave is a circular tablet in memory of his father, Ernest Betjeman (1872-1934).

The font was found buried beneath the floor during the 1864 renovations and is carved from sandstone. It resembles the font at Porthilly Church and was probably made by the same craftsmen. The bowl and base are c. 1080, but the plinth is modern.

Near the font is a carved chest which is very old, being listed in the church inventory of 1613. The nave is separated from the chancel by the remains of a finely carved screen, the top of which was crudely cut off during the period when the church was being buried by the encroaching sand.

Once there were two bells in the tower, one being inscribed Alfredus Rex. Alfred was King of England from AD 871 to 899 and this suggests that the church was substantial enough to have a bell tower in those remote days. Legend has it that the bell was sold to either St Eval or St Ervan parishes across the estuary, and that whilst being transported the boat was nearly swamped. Maybe it still lies beneath the shifting sands of the river, for there is no record of it being received in either of those parishes. The present bell is incribed 'Sahel' and was bought in 1875 from the wreck of the Italian vessel *Immacolata*, which was wrecked off Greenaway. The name implies that it belonged to an older ship.

A morning service together with Holy Communion held on the nearest Sunday to September 29th is known as 'Little Sunday', for the Feast of St Michael and All Angels. For many years it was the only morning service held in the church. Today morning communions are held at Christmas, Easter, Whitsun and during the summer holiday weeks when many visitors attend.

St Enodoc church has also its niche in the realms of fiction, for it was here that Judith, the heroine of Sabine Baring-Gould's novel *In the Roar of the Sea* married the villainous 'Cruel Coppinger'.

As we leave the church, we note the weathered slate memorial slab fixed against the right-hand side of the inner wall of the porch. It once covered the table tomb of John Mably, who was buried on July 24th, 1687, and his daughter Alice who followed him a week later on July 30th. Crudely carved figures of father and daughter with their hands crossed over their breasts are faintly visible, and a long epitaph follows, the closing lines of which read:

> My wife and I did in love
> So well agree.
> Yet must I part for God
> Would have it so to be
> From my wife Ann Mably.

Beside the churchyard path is a collection of medieval domestic mortars and stoups used for grinding corn. They have no religious significance but were the collection of a Cornish lady who obtained them from various parts of the country and presented them to the vicar, who placed them in their present position. It is said that he bored a hole in the bottom of each vessel because he did not like to see rainwater standing in them.

The churchyard contains graves of unknown sailors, whose ships were wrecked on the notorious Doom Bar. Some of the graves have been found to be two or three tiers deep.

Joanna, the young wife of Malachi Martyn, who died on March 16th, 1824, aged 22, left an omnibus request to all her family to care for her children. Her gravestone reads:

> My husband and my father dear
> I take farewell of you.
> My brother and my sister dear
> I bid you all adieu.
> My children dear I leave behind
> My friends relieve their wants
> And for my sake for them provide,
> For they are tender plants.

As we leave this lonely acre, be it spring or summer, we look for a moment beyond the tamarisks to the dunes and marram grass, to the last trembling clusters of sea pinks and tight beds of purple thyme; listen to the click of golf ball to club and the distant buzz of voices, and to the soaring silver trilling of an invisible skylark; you will be transported to that magic world of living sounds which was so faithfully pictured by a faithful friend of Cornwall, who rests nearby. In autumn, watch the changing hues of sunset over Hawker's Cove on the Padstow side, and on a winter's day as you shelter against the stone hedges while breakers surge over the Doom Bar and foam flies white across the dunes, maybe you will hear the voices of long dead sailors and the crash of splintering masts. Imagination? Of course! But the scene will have done something to evoke those echoes from the past.

ST MINVER TO ROCK

St Minver Churchtown

ST MINVER Churchtown, where four roads intersect, is the hub of this large parish. From the east comes the road from Wadebridge; from the north, Portquin and Port Isaac; from the west, the road from Polzeath, Porthilly, Rock and Tredrizzick. The fourth turning is into a short lane leading up from the church and vicarage. The Fourways Inn and Church of St Menefreda are the main buildings here.

Almost the whole of the village came up for sale on July 13th, 1925, when the Sandford-owned St Minver Estate was auctioned at the Town Hall, Wadebridge. Some 772 acres comprising 5 mixed farms, 16 cottages, the Post Office, various business premises, accommodation land and building sites were sold.

The Fourways Inn, previously named the Four Turnings, has had a long and colourful association with the parish. At one stage the innkeeper lost his licence due to out-of-hours drinking and rowdiness. On another occasion a local imbiber is reputed to have bitten off the head of a live rat for a bet.

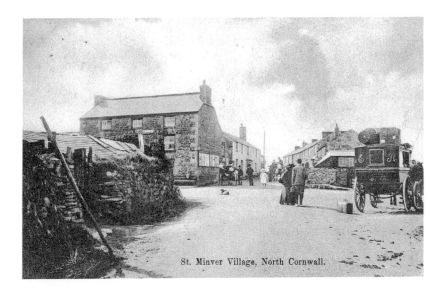

St. Minver Village, North Cornwall.

21.   The Temperance Inn, St Minver, about 1910

In 1854 the inn was turned into a temperance hotel, in the hope of attracting a better class of trade during a rise in Wesleyan Methodism, and in 1890 it was named the Temperance Inn. In 1956 Squadron Leader Joe Mercer was serving in the RAF in Cornwall, and during this period bought the pub as a house. He realised the potential of the site and in 1962 opened the pub, now named Fourways, and remained there as landlord until his recent retirement. His son Jamie then took over the reins of what has become one of the most popular pubs in the area.

Mr Mercer is an ardent fan of his home football team, Blackburn Rovers, and has many times made the round 365 mile journey to watch them play at Ewood Park, their home ground. Team members have stayed at Fourways during the summer months, and the bar walls bear many photographs and memorabilia of the team.

Fourways has been considerably renovated, a bar restaurant extension added, with a launderette and a squash court nearby.

The Church of St Menefreda

How pleasant it is to walk past the ancient stone cottages which flank the eastern lychgate of St Minver church and to wander slowly through the ranks of leaning slate tombstones to the southern porch of this delightful church! It is dedicated to St Menefreda, supposedly one of the twenty-four children of the Welsh King Brechan. In many parts of Cornwall Christian churches have been built on the sites of pagan altars, and this church is one of them. Crude slate coffins of pre-Christian burials have come to light in the churchyard.

The first church stood here in Saxon times, but no evidence of its construction remains; no doubt it was wooden and rebuilt several times. The first vicar was recorded in 1255, and the church was the mother church with chapels at St Enodoc and Porthilly. Some parishioners have names going back 400 years in the parish registers.

The church comprises chancel, nave, south aisle and porch. The slightly leaning spire on the thirteenth-century remodelled west broached tower is a landmark for miles around and stands 120 feet above ground, 330 feet above sea level.

We enter through the fourteenth-century south porch of which only the original wagon roof remains. Above the entrance is an old slate sundial. About two feet above the door handle on the stone arch is a small consecration cross carved when the rebuilding was completed.

The wooden stocks are over 500 years old and were last used at the end of the nineteenth century for the punishment of two orchard-robbing boys who were clapped in, with their father's written consent, to prevent them being fined at Petty Sessions.

Inside the door, a few feet along the wall, is a richly carved 'half capital' stone mounted on an oak pedestal. It was discovered in July 1927 when plaster was removed from the east wall, and the rough back of the embedded stone became visible. The stone is completely different from any other stonework in the church and was suggested by experts at South Kensington Museum to be the top half of a pillar piscina. There could be some doubt regarding this as the bowl is much larger and hardly smooth enough when compared with other pillared piscinas.

As we cross to the north aisle we note the carved doors to the belfry tower. They are all that remain of the once gilded and painted chancel screen. Around 1820 the dilapidated screen was stored in an outhouse in the grounds of St Minver House where it lay for about fifty years until rediscovered and sent to church restorers at Poole in Dorset who repainted and adapted it for its present position.

The fifteenth-century pew backs and ends include carvings of Adam and Eve and Henry VII and are worth close examination.

The slate octagonal pillars and arches of the north aisle are unusual for Cornwall.

On the north wall is a badly-damaged slate front panel of the tomb chest of Elizabeth and Thomas Stone, who died in 1586 and 1604 respectively. The kneeling figure of Thomas has lost all its detail down to the waist, but his well-designed breeches with S motif embroidery are intact, as is his prayer cushion, but detail has flaked from the legs. Elizabeth is in better shape and wears a hat and ruff. Her gown has elaborate shoulders and V front, and she wears a chain with ornamental cross. Thomas hailed from Trevigoe near Port Quin, and Elizabeth from Hayne.

Behind the pulpit is the top half of a stone spiral staircase which led up to the rood screen.

Sometimes the departed left some sort of bequest to the parish, and on the north wall can be seen a well-preserved incised lettered tablet in memory of John Randall who died on July 23rd, 1733. In his will he bequeathed ten shillings to the Minister of St Minver church to preach a funeral sermon annually on the Feast of St John the Evangelist for the term of 1,000 years. He also bequeathed twenty shillings a year to be distributed by the Minister, Wardens and Overseers for a similar period to the poor widows and fatherless children of the parish. These two sums were to be payable by the tenants of Mismeer in St Minver parish. Over 250 years have elapsed since those bequests were made, and if still carried out, would continue until the year 2733. John Randall evidently intended that his name would not be lost for a long time, but happily for church officials and relatives, the income has died.

The altar rails are from the era of Queen Anne and at one time were removed and lost. In 1925 a search was made in a nearby barn where it was known that materials from a previous restoration were stored, and joinery matching exactly the remnants still in position were found, restored and refixed.

In the chancel and sanctuary is a memorial to John Roe of Trewornan, erected by Thomas Darell, Sheriff of Cornwall in 1666.

On the floor of the south aisle is a beautiful brass memorial to Roger Opy who stands with his hands emerging from the voluminous sleeves of a fur-lined mantle; his fingertips touch his breast, and he wears long, bobbed hair. The inscription in Latin when translated reads:

Here lies the body of Roger Opy son of Richard Opy and Elizabeth his wife who was the daughter of John Carminow, Knight, who died the 13 day of January in the year of our Lord 1517 on whose soul may God have mercy. I shall not die but live and declare the works of the Lord.

The glass in the east window has lovely colours and was produced in 1870 by O'Connor of London.

On the west wall of the south aisle is King Charles II's letter of thanks and coat of arms, now cleaned and restored. Alongside is a verbatim transcript of the letter.

Tragedy is also recorded on a plaque:

In memory of Charles Symons son of Henry and Mary Ann Symons who was born at Roserrow in this parish on 3 January 1840, Master of the ship Pendragon of Liverpool who was washed overboard during a hurricane in the Indian Ocean on 12 March 1896 in the 36th year of his age.

Note the brass commemorating the restoration of the church in 1872:

This church was restored AD 1872 and the entire rebuilding of the tower and spire (which was in a falling state) was commenced AD 1874 and completed AD 1875 under the directions of Architect James Piers St Aubyn, Esq., of Temple, London.

St Aubyn was one of the most notorious and ruthless restorers of churches and gutted several in Cornwall with little regard to their antiquity. No doubt he had difficulties to contend with and was probably limited in his choice of materials, but the south aisle pews in contrast to the old pews are uncomfortable and ugly. He could have used Delabole slate for re-laying the floor but instead he substituted Minton floor tiles in chequerboard pattern, which are completely out of keeping in this church. He also restored St Enodoc and Porthilly Churches, and among other churches which received his ministrations were Camborne, St Keverne, Maker, Gulval and Minster, to mention but a few.

J. Bosankoe, the local poet of whom more details are given elsewhere, waxed lyrical when the renovations were under way:

> In eighteen hundred and seventy one
> The restoring of the church was on.
> It was not finished in that date –
> It took some time to renovate.
>
> The seats and screens there too, we find
> St Aubyn gave the grand design;
> For centuries there the pillars stood –
> Come stranger – view the hand of God.

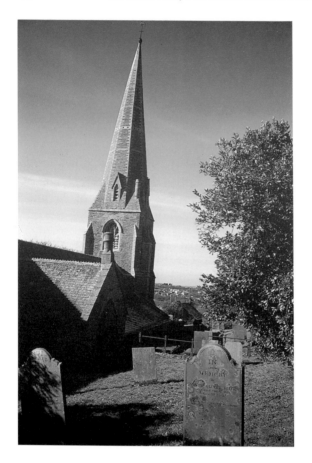

22. The twisted
spire of St
Menefreda

Now organ too of lovely sound,
It cost more than three hundred pound
And now, new spire there we find
The bells and music so subline.

A copy of the 1717 'Vinegar Bible' is held by the church.
Printed by a John Baskett, it contained so many mistakes that
it has been dubbed 'a basketful of errors', of which the misprint
in verse 2 chapter xx of St Luke reads 'the parable of the
vinegar' instead of 'the vineyard'.

The churchyard is large, with the newer area extending northwards where there is another lychgate incorporating a Cornish stile instead of gates.

The old lichen-crusted memorials in the lower churchyard are fascinating and worth examining. Near the south porch is a cross, and on this side of the churchyard is a 'palimpsest' stone – one whose back commemorates a different person from the front owing to its having been reversed.

In 1859 it came to light that the Sexton was in the habit of privately burying the bodies of illegitimate children at night without informing the Vicar. A woman from St Endellion came to St Minver for confinement, put the dead infant into a box and paid the Sexton one shilling for its disposal.

Culled at random from the many epitaphs are the following. Samuel Sleeman was only sixteen years of age when he died and is likened to a flower:

Today the flower bloweth and spreadeth forth its leaves
And we admire its beauty but the glory is short
And it soon fadeth and falls to the ground.

Eleanor and William Lagoe, Honor Cook and her brother all lie together near the south-west corner of the churchyard, and their epitaph is identical to that for Nicholas and Barbara Thomas at St Kew, except for the relationship:

Here lieth the husband and the wife
A sister and a brother who
Friendly neighbours were to all
A pattern for all others;
No oath nor lyes nor passions fire
By them were preached abroad
But when afflicting trials came
Resigned their wills to God.
They truly served the Lord above
Were just to all mankind
Before grim Death did call them home
A better place to find.

23.   The Quaker Burial Ground

From St Minver Churchtown To Rock via Tredrissick, Pityme and Rock Road

From Fourways Inn we turn left, passing the higher churchyard and lychgate on our left. At the T-junction we continue bearing left past Trevanger Farm and continue downhill to Tredrissick Bridge. But before going on, there is a diversion for those interested in the past. About 700 yards along the right-hand fork leading to New Polzeath is the old Quaker Burial Ground, on the left-hand side of the road between Park Farm and Treglines Farm.

At the end of the seventeenth century there were many Quakers in St Minver parish. They had a Meeting House at Treglines but today no trace of it remains. The burial ground is surrounded by a high wall. The Parish Register for the years 1696 to 1745 records twenty-eight Quaker burials, but by 1808 the sect was extinct. John Peters (1645-1708), an eminent Quaker minister, is buried here. For many years Peters was Steward under Sir John Carew of Roserrow and joined the Quakers in 1672. His views brought him imprisonment on several occasions when he refused to pay tithes and would not take the Oath of Allegiance. The burial ground is now overgrown with trees. Among the undergrowth in springtime white ramson flowers bring a strong whiff of garlic through this desolate enclosure. As summer comes, the ramsons give way to bowers of red campions. Nature has come into her own, and there are no visible headstones to trace the resting places of those long-departed Quakers in this abandoned God's Acre.

Returning to Tredrissick Bridge we continue up the hill through Tredrissick village. There are a few old dwellings: a Wesleyan Methodist Chapel, Primary School, a store with off-licence, and a butcher. Considerable development and infilling have recently taken place.

1847 was a year of 'Evangelical Revival' in Cornwall, and shortly afterwards twenty converts were recorded after a month's services at Tredrissick. The chapel appears to have been enlarged between 1835 and 1854 when part of Chapel Meadow was conveyed to the trustees. In 1838 the society was prospering and sixty-three more members were added. At one revival meeting Mary Brabyn Gray, a member of the Trelights Chapel, reported that she saw 'sinners falling like Dagon before the Ark'. 'Mutual Improvement Classes' were held after revivals to attain 'Christian perfection' and many people progressed a long way on that road. It was said of William Male of Tredrissick (1786-1865) 'It is no use to speak of anybody's faults to William Male, for either he believes they have none, or that we have no right to speak of them'. The interiors of many chapels were austere, but at Tredrissick age added mellowness and the furnishings added something of distinction.

At Pityme, also considerably developed, is a Business Centre which contains a plant hire service, a long-established garage,

24.   On the Rock Road in the early 1900s

a joinery works, a builder's merchant; insurance facilities, garden machinery sales and service, a well known firm of boatbuilders, watersports sales and service, and vacant units available for further businesses.

We proceed along the wide stretch of Rock Road, passing the Pityme Inn on our left – a free house and pleasant stopping place for the thirsty, where bar snacks, lunches and evening meals are served all year round.

A right-hand fork leads to Trebetherick and Polzeath. Private dwellings on each side of the Rock Road illustrate the scourge of pre-war ribbon development as we approach Splatt. Much infilling has now taken place and a road on the left leads into Penmayne.

Interspersed among the houses are several business premises that provide services for this semi-rural and tourist-oriented part of St Minver parish: a small supermarket, garage, household and leisure stores, TV and electrical services, estate agents, where the prices of local properties are now surely

25.   Rock Methodist Chapel in the 1990s

platinum-edged; also excellent residential and nursing homes for the retired, the elderly and the convalescent.

We now approach crossroads where the right fork leads to Trebetherick and Polzeath and joins the fork road from Pityme. The left fork joins the Penmayne road.

We continue past the post office and Rock Methodist Chapel on our right. Here the road curves past old cottages, many of which have been extended and modernised.

The final half mile is past tree-girt properties to Rock village where the road skirts the beach and ends at the public car park.   But let us return for a moment to the signpost on our left marked Porthilly and walk down the steep narrow lane, flanked with high Cornish hedges and topped by shady trees, until the wide stretch of the Camel estuary and Padstow come into view beyond Porthilly Cove.

ST ENODOC TO TREBETHERICK AND POLZEATH

St Enodoc Church to Daymer Bay, Greenaway and Trebetherick

FROM the lychgate of St Enodoc church we head west, following the left-hand path which skirts the 12th fairway and green, swinging round into the curve of Daymer Bay.

The right fork of the path leads to the end of a *cul-de-sac*, passing a few tree-surrounded residences including the late Sir John Betjeman's detached cottage Treen, which was his Cornish home for thirty years and the setting of much of his writing. In the early 1990s the cottage and its grounds were on the market at the asking price of a quarter of a million pounds.

Daymer Bay lies beneath the shadow of Bray Hill and is sheltered from north winds by the cliffs of Greenaway. It has a splendid line of flat golden estuary sand.

Across the estuary are St George's Well beach, Gun Point, Harbour Cove and, crowned by the Daymark stack, Stepper Point. The remains of a submerged forest can sometimes be seen at low tide near the Doom Bar off Daymer Bay.

During World War II Daymer Bay was protected from

26.   Stepper Point and Newland Island from Rock

invasion by a high metal screen built across the beach; barbed wire entanglements were placed along the frontage and the sand dunes were planted with mines. Danger notices were prominently displayed but several dogs were blown up (unfortunately dogs do not read) and there was one human tragedy when a foolhardy young aircraftsman home on leave was dared by his two sisters to cross the minefield and was blown to pieces.

Before we cross the beach and continue along the coastal footpath to Greenaway, let us divert to Daymer Lane. This narrow, winding road starts from the road junction above Trebetherick Post Office and dips down past the tree-girt houses to the dead end above the beach, where there is a large car park, shop and café. Daymer Lane, like several other lanes on the Padstow side of the Camel estuary, was a 'sanding lane', and was used extensively by farmers who, within living memory, loaded sand into carts and spread it upon their fields as a fertilizer, for it contains a high percentage of calcium carbonate in its grains. During holiday periods this road has traffic problems for residents and visitors, and Stop! Go! reverse, smile, and patience are the keywords.

Around the 1830s there were several cottages on the left-hand side of Daymer Lane. Their parlours faced south for sun and warmth, and their back doors opened onto the lane. The gardens behind their front walls were sheltered from the north winds, but by the 1850s most of these dwellings had disappeared. Today there is a very different scene; larger expensive residences cover this once-rural habitat and, as at Rock, several are holiday homes for the affluent although there is a fair proportion of resident locals and immigrants. Just off the main road on the left from Rock to Polzeath is the long-established St Moritz Hotel. The recent facelift to the public rooms area and the creation of the Laureate's Restaurant, named after Sir John Betjeman, would have been visited and I hope approved by him for its décor, cuisine and service. Further developments in the way of sporting facilities and holiday units form a complex around the hotel buildings.

Back now to Greenaway where we can walk over its grassy clifftops. It is a great misfortune that the waters of this lovely estuary have been badly polluted in recent years by the mismanagement of a succession of sewage schemes since the 1960s. But on a fine summer day at low tide one can still look down on the golden sand of the Doom Bar mingling with the blue water of the Camel River and the Atlantic Ocean.

Greenaway was immortalised by Betjeman's poem of that name, in which he describes the breezy cliff, withered sea pinks and an awkward stile which leads down to a small smelly bay, where he listens to the dragging roar of breakers and the hissing surf.

Greenaway is dotted with a number of elegant pre-war houses with white walls, steep slated roofs with dormers and small paned windows. They are mainly in keeping with the Cornish landscape, although the building at Trebetherick detracts sadly from the grandeur of the view towards Pentire Point from the Padstow side of the estuary. Behind, more modern bungalows have sprung up on the estates; the roads in some instances are unsurfaced and in winter can be horrific for small cars.

Jesus Well

FROM St Enodoc Church or from the footbridge that I have previously mentioned an interesting detour up the unfenced road can be made for some three quarters of a mile to Jesus Well, which is situated about 400 yards from the left-hand verge.

A small stone building with a pitched roof and open arched doorway in the gable end stands over the well in which grow lush ferns and vegetation. A rough niche stands at the end of the well, possibly to hold a drinking vessel, crucifix or effigy. It was once the centre of long-distance pilgrimages by those who believed its waters possessed healing powers.

On one occasion in 1876 a boatman's wife named Mary Cranwell who suffered from erysipelas, an acute skin inflammation, knelt by the well, recited the Litany and bathed the diseased parts three times in the waters. After the third immersion, the inflammation disappeared.

Children with whooping cough were taken there to drink, and pins and money were dropped into the waters for telling fortunes. In 1778 gales shifted the sands near the well and a chapel and cemetery were exposed together with slate coffins, human bones, spoons, rings and other ornaments. Today no traces of chapel or Churchyard can be seen.

Greenaway to Polzeath

WE continue our walk along the cliff to Broadagogue Cove and Greenaway Point, where the wide inlet of Polzeath Bay comes into view.

Polzeath is split into two parts – the old and the new, both overlooking a magnificent stretch of golden sand between Pentire Head to the north and Highcliff to the west.

Old Polzeath village lies at the foot of two roads – one entering from St Minver to the north-east and the other from Rock and Trebetherick to the south. Here are sited the Post Office and shops, overlooked by a hill covered by modern housing, and behind the shops, a wooded valley with a caravan park leading up to Shilla Mill. The road skirts the beach, winding up the hill to New Polzeath and away to the hinterland of the parish to join the Pendogget-Delabole road.

Across the beach to the north-east is New Polzeath with its cliff frontage of stone-built Edwardian houses, post-World War I semi-bungalows and, extending behind them, the considerable development that followed World War II.

Polzeath Bay displays a huge expanse of sand at low tide and is a family paradise for holidaymakers. Bathing is safe, but it is wise to remember that the Atlantic Ocean must always be treated with respect, for it can be your best friend or your worst enemy. This unspoilt beach produces wonderful surfing when the wind-whipped rollers come thundering in, while on mild days there is only a gentle rhythmic surge of waves slapping the rippled furrows of sand.

During the summer of 1796 the villagers must have been surprised to find a dead whale sixty-five feet long washed up on the beach. However, good use was made of its unexpected odorous carcase, which was cut up and carried away to be used as manure. From its bones a small structure called Whale House was constructed in the grounds of St Minver House.

In January 1866 the *Juliet*, laden with a cargo of rum and sugar, was wrecked in the Camel estuary and much of her cargo washed into Polzeath Bay. 280 casks of rum out of 400 were recovered, but none of the sugar. Over-proof rum mixed with seawater that was found in hollows in the rocks was scooped out and drunk. A great deal of drunkenness followed, and a St Austell man drank so much that he died, despite the arrival of a doctor with a stomach pump.

THE POST OFFICE & POLZEATH BAY.

27.   Old Post Office, Polzeath, about 1914

28.   Polzeath in the 1900s

In 1949 Polzeath beach was featured in a J. Arthur Rank film as a Scottish bay in the £300,000 production of *Madeleine*, a story of the famous 1857 murder trial of Madeleine Smith. The film starred Norman Wooland and Ann Todd, with her first husband David Lean as director. The script called for a wide beach with heavy breaking seas, and Miss Todd had to ride across it, during which time the horse would bolt and Miss Todd would ride straight into the sea and be rescued by Wooland, playing the part of her French lover. During rehearsals, the horse actually bolted and the actress was carried across the beach hanging on to the pommel of the saddle. Unfortunately, holidaymakers in bathing costumes could be seen in the background and the scene was reshot using Miss Todd's understudy, for the star was too shocked to attempt a repeat performance.

Much of the sand along the North Cornwall coast contains a high proportion of calcium carbonate, and farmers regularly brought their carts, usually drawn by two horses, to the beach where they loaded up this valuable fertilizer and spread it on their fields.

During World War II tank traps were built along the beach entrance by the bridge. These golden acres have also lured several vehicles to destruction when their owners, miscalculating the speed of the incoming tide, have found they had parked their cars too far out. Despite frantic efforts to move them by ropes and tractors, they have been immersed, presenting sad sights when the tide ebbed.

Over 140 years ago tourism began to show in Polzeath, and an advertisement in the *West Briton* of April 30th, 1847 read:

To let immediately, either by the week or month, Furnished seaside lodgings, in a house recently built for the accommodation of Gentry at that delightful and favorite resort of Polseath [sic] Beach in the parish of St Minver, in the County of Cornwall which commands a most beautiful and picturesque view of the North Sea Coast. The house contains five excellent bedrooms, three parlours, Kitchen and other conveniences.

About seventy years later, in the early 1920s, hoteliers waxed lyrical in their brochures. One issued by Trevose View tells us that:

... at no point has Nature dealt more bountifully than at Polseath and its surroundings ... all may find here much to interest and all that will conduce to health of body and mind. The pure breezes direct from the Atlantic are considered the most invigorating in the West of England. The beach is the largest, cleanest and finest in Cornwall ... and for tennis, cycling and driving it is not surpassed as its sands are so firm that the heaviest conveyances make but little impression ... the aged, infirm and tired can sit within the house and have full view of the beach and ocean ... we cannot offer Society other than Nature's charms ... we cannot offer entertainment of Pier or Band ... no Minstrels other than the song of larks mingled with the ceaseless monotone of the sea. Polseath is simply an ideal place where the world ceases from troubling, and the weary can find rest.

And the charge for staying in this paradise which provided everything except table linen, silver and cutlery?

May 3 guineas per week,
June $3\frac{1}{2}$ guineas,
July 5 guineas
August and September 6 guineas
October $2\frac{1}{2}$ guineas

Atlantic Terrace at that time consisted of seven houses, among which was Atlantic House. From its proprietors' tariff we glean that friends to lunch cost two shillings; if they stayed to tea the charge was sixpence, and three shillings and sixpence for dinner. Hot baths were sixpence a bath, and cold ones two shillings per week. Morning tea cost threepence; a fire in your bedroom was one shilling and sixpence per day, or sixpence if lit only in the evening; if you brought your dog it cost you five shillings per week. Photographers who processed their own material could have the use of a darkroom for ninepence per hour, plus threepence per minute after the hour. Oh for those halcyon days!

Polzeath Methodist Church

THE year 1884 saw a religious revival at Tredrissick and, following that, weekly class meetings to satisfy the spiritual needs of those who had joined the Methodist Movement were held at Polzeath under the leadership of Mr John Mably. After some weeks it became obvious that a Sunday service was necessary, and on Easter Sunday of that year one took place in a building called the Account House, an adjunct to a local mine. This building served as the first Polzeath Post Office during the years 1913 to 1936, after which it became a private residence.

1898 saw the rental of a plot of land for the erection of a more suitable building for worship, and on August Bank Holiday of that year a timber-framed building was consecrated. Locally known as The Tabernacle, it remained in use until 1932, when road widening brought about its demise.

On April 15th, 1933 Mr Haynes, the sole survivor of the original chapel trustees, handed over his authority to a newly-elected Trust Committee when the ever-increasing popularity of Polzeath with visitors necessitated the building of a new church hall, to replace the recently-demolished Methodist Church, on a unique site overlooking the beach and Pentire Head.

A spacious building with ample storage room in the basement was later erected by the builders Messrs Hart & Job.

29. Polzeath in the 1990s

30. Mr S. H. Lander was a cycle agent in the area

NEW POLZEATH TO PENTIRE POINT AND LUNDY BAY TO PORT QUIN

New Polzeath to the Rumps and Pentire Point

FROM the eastern end of Polzeath beach we pick up the coastal footpath that leads in front of the gardens of the row of large semi-bungalows to the New Polzeath car park. Here we turn right, then right again into Gulland Road and on to Baby Beach Lane. Now we ascend a flight of wooden steps onto National Trust land where we turn left at the head of Breakneck Cavern. We then take the right-hand branch on rising ground beside field hedges and through a gateway into the lane which leads into the yard of Pentire Farm.

Pentire Farm, also owned by the National Trust, has a car park to serve motorists arriving from the St Endellion-New Polzeath road. From this point it is a pleasant walk out to the Rumps and Pentire Point.

In 1935 when the farm was put on the market a disaster could have occurred, for a layout was envisaged whereby the fields were to be split up and sold for development into scores of building sites. A similar tragedy almost occurred at Booby's Bay and Trevose Head further down the coast. Public reaction to this despoilation was immediate, and a national appeal was launched to buy the land for the National Trust. This was successful and since then gifts and acquisitions have secured all the land to the north of the road to Polzeath. Pentire Glaze Farm is now farmed with Pentire, and the farmhouse and cottages are used for holiday lettings.

From Pentire farmyard we head towards the Rumps, turning right along a tamarisk hedge until we again pick up the coastal footpath. Below is Sandinway Beach and an enormous cavern known as Coppinger's Cave, but it is difficult to visualize how any smuggler could have stored contraband in it.

The Rumps cliff castle, or promontory fort, is a splendid example of a stronghold in which natural features were utilized for defence by the Iron Age people. There is a gap in the outer rampart which has been made into a sheep hedge. The entrance is probably the original one, and the path through it leads to the two inner ramparts. At one time they could have been much higher, but centuries of erosion have caused the earth and stone to slide down into their ditches, which have now become partially filled and grass covered.

These Iron Age people were crafty in their selection of this isolated headland with high cliffs that almost surround their encampment, for it saved them much labour in building ramparts which were needed only along the narrow headland neck, while the ditch from which they were quarried faced landwards. So it can be seen that a coastal stronghold was created with a minimum of effort, with commanding views on all sides.

During 1966-1969 excavatory work was carried out by the Cornwall Archaeological Society. The lee sides of the ramparts were found to have been used by the occupants as living quarters, and bones of domestic animals, seashells and pottery came to light.

From the summit of the Rumps we look down onto Sevensouls Rock and further out to sea, the Mouls, a small rocky islet.

From Rumps Point we pick up the coastal footpath again

and head south, passing magnificent rock scenery all the way to Pentire Point. The whole of this headland is an excellent place to enjoy cliff flowers in spring and summer, when primroses, squills, cowslips, bluebells, thrift, yellow kidney vetch, lesser birdsfoot trefoil and the trembling white bladder campion are in bloom. Orange-gold gorse cascades down the cliff sides, which are riddled with caves. Later come red and white valerian, red campions, foxgloves, the drooping pink flower heads of the musk thistle and carpets of purple wild thyme. On the cliff edges rock samphire and sea lavender bloom.

On a summer day when waves ride high into Polzeath and Lundy bays after an overnight storm, one can hear the boom of surf in distant blowholes. Gulls fly high, and the air quivers with the trilling of unseen skylarks. In places the cliffs break into strange arches and pinnacles, and in others they plunge down in sheer precipices to the sea.

Among the birds which can be seen here are rock and meadow pipits, stonechats, wheatears, linnets, ravens, jackdaws, feral pigeons, buzzards, kestrels and sparrowhawks.

The small rocky island of Newland (called Puffin Island by the pleasure-boat operators of Padstow), rises some 165 feet from the sea and is about one mile in circumference. It is a haven for grey seals; often, a few puffins and numerous cormorants can be seen drying their outstretched wings in the sun. In the nineteenth century parties sometimes visited this rock in summer to shoot seabirds and, on occasions when sudden storms arose, both ladies and gentlemen found themselves confined on this inhospitable surface for several days without getting any assistance from the shore.

It was on Pentire Point that Lawrence Binyon, the poet, wrote the immortal words that echo through the Royal Albert Hall in London at the climax of the annual Festival of Remembrance to those who died in the two World Wars and more recently, the Falklands operation:

> They shall not grow old as we that are left grow old
> Age shall not weary them, nor the years condemn.

At the going down of the sun, and in the morning
We shall remember them.

This fierce coastline has romantic tales of smugglers and wrecking, and it was at Pentire Glaze that the Reverend Sabine Baring-Gould set the scene for his ever-green novel *In the Roar of the Sea* , with Cruel Coppinger the villain and Judith Trevisa the heroine. There is speculation as to the identify of Coppinger; where he came from, and where he settled. The Reverend Stephen Hawker, the eccentric vicar of Morwenstow who, like Baring-Gould, was sometimes given to flights of fancy, claimed that Coppinger landed and lived near Morwenstow, and Baring-Gould admitted that he moved the smuggler's location further west.

It appears that Curll Coppinger was a Dane who landed during a storm, the vessel in which he travelled having vanished. He met a farmer's daughter who was riding on a mule and forced her to take him to her father's farm. Coppinger remained in the area for several years, during which time he gathered around him a gang of smugglers and wreckers, and operated from his lugger *The Black Prince*. The local folk soon realised the true character of this stranger for he was merciless to anyone who crossed his path, and they gave him the name 'Cruel Coppinger'. It is said that he beheaded a Customs official on the gunwhale of his boat as a warning to others. His departure was as mysterious as his arrival, for during a storm a strange ship appeared; a small boat came ashore, Coppinger stepped into it, boarded the waiting vessel, and was never seen again. This legend, from which Baring-Gould produced his novel, could be in part a fragment of a folk memory from the days of the Danish invaders.

According to Miss M.A. Courtenay in her book *Cornish Feasts and Folklore*, the real Coppinger at one time amassed enough money by smuggling to buy a small estate near the sea, the title deeds of which, signed with his name, still exist. However, in his old age, Coppinger was reduced to poverty and subsisted on charity.

From Pentire Point the footpath takes us into the curve of Padstow Bay, with the flat sands and surf of Hayle Bay and New and Old Polzeath on either side. Above Breakneck Cavern we rejoin our original route back to Pentire Haven (Baby Beach), via the flight of wooden steps.

Lundy Bay to Port Quin

Next to the lay-by below Tremanis, which is a large house on the left-hand side of the road that leads to New Polzeath from the St Minver-Port Quin crossroads, is the National Trust car park for Lundy Bay, which can only be reached on foot.

We cross the road and join the signposted footpath which winds gently down through fields that skirt woodland of oak, ash, holly, hawthorn and blackthorn to the cliffs about ten minutes walk below. But it is pleasant to dawdle and occasionally halt, to admire the wild flowers and shrubs of the season: dog rose, bramble, honeysuckle, coltsfoot, lesser celandine, cuckoo pint, teasel, rosebay willowherb, foxglove and a host of other blooms.

Now the path winds down to Lundy Bay where shelves of smooth rock end in sand. Bathing is good but it is advisable to keep a frequent eye on the incoming tide when exploring the nearby caves and caverns. Being trapped here so far away from human habitation could be an unpleasant, if not fatal, experience.

As we approach the cliff edge, a spectacular natural rock arch comes into view, created many years ago when a sea-carved cave collapsed.

This is a coast where smuggled goods were landed, and there was once a hidden way up from the shore, now vanished beneath bushes and undergrowth.

From the beach we follow the path that winds steeply upwards to Pennywilgie Point and turns inwards as Epphaven

31.   Doyden Castle

Cove comes into view below. The small cave-like hole on the right of the path is an adit from an old mine working.

We ford a small stream at the head of the cove and climb upwards to Trevan Point, where the footpath continues outside a stone hedge. Down below are Pigeon and Gilson's Coves.

There are a number of old mine shafts in this area which should be approached with great care. A fenced-off square shaft on the cliff edge is part of a nineteenth-century antimony mine, the adit of which runs into another cave at Port Quin.

We are now approaching Doyden Point where, perched on a small headland, sits a folly known as Doyden Castle. The land upon which it is built was bought for £500 by a Captain Conor. In 1839 Samuel Seymour of Gonvena House, Wadebridge, decided to build the mini-castle as a retreat where he could enjoy solitude or alternatively, dining, drinking and dicing with his friends. Evidence of his occupation can be seen

32.   Carnweather and Daymer Points

in the wine bins on the lower floor. Arriving by gig, he drove it round the track on the cliff side of his domain so that when he was ready to return home, the horse would be facing the return track on the inland side of the headland. The folly appeared in the popular *Poldark* television saga a few years ago, where it was used as the house of Dr Ennis. The building is now owned by the National Trust and can be rented – if one is not averse to the curiosity of tourists peeping through the latticed windows.

The view from Doyden is magnificent when we stop and look westward, back to Trevan and Carnweather Points, shielding Lundy Bay. Beyond is Com Head with the Rumps rising up in the distance, and seawards the dark bulk of the Mouls rock. On December 5th, 1979 the 2,800 ton Greek freighter *Skopelos Sky* drove onto the rocks below Doyden in a storm and broke into three pieces.

The track from Doyden Castle winds back to Doyden House, built as a retirement home for a former Governor of Wandsworth Gaol. It is also now owned by the National Trust and its outbuildings have been converted into holiday accommodation.

After leaving the car park we reach the lane that drops down steeply into the hamlet of Port Quin, which huddles at the head of a narrow inlet with Killan Head towering above it on the eastern side. The headland is privately owned, but it can be reached by walking through Port Quin and following the valley road up past the group of cottages where, on the left, a public footpath leads up to the headland and more spectacular views.

There have been several variations of the name Port Quin. A parish record of 1327 during the reign of Edward III mentions Laurence de Porquin, a local who took his name from the parish. In 1415 a record mentions Thomas Portquyn. In Elizabethan times it was referred to as Parquin. In St Endellion churchyard the tombstone of Catharine Delamore, dated 1752, refers to it as Port Quin. Other variations were Port Guin and Porth Guynne. Translated, it means 'the white port' and probably originated from the fact that in this area slate flecked with white was quarried.

Port Quin relied greatly on its fishing industry, as can be seen by the size of its old fish cellars, now converted into private holiday units, lying on the left of the hairpin bend at the foot of the hill. Inshore seining and drag netting were the usual methods of fishing in those days. Coal and manure were also unloaded here, and it is said that granite stone shipped from Lundy Island in the Bristol Channel was also brought here and taken up to St Endellion church for the construction of the tower.

Port Quin miners operated the Doyden antimony mine during the last century and, when mining became uneconomic, many inhabitants emigrated to Canada so that the hamlet remained almost empty for a generation. This gave rise to various colourful legends.

The most popular story sets out that Port Quin was a prosperous fishing village until one Sunday when the boats put out to sea. A tremendous storm blew up and the fishing boats were smashed to pieces on the treacherous rocks of Lundy Bay. The broken-hearted dependents and their families gathered up their belongings and left their cottages, never to return. Only the very old were left, and when they died, so did the hamlet. A colourful story, but one without a shred of proof. The legend was further enhanced when Fred Bramley, the artist, exhibited a painting at the Tate Gallery entitled *A Hopeless Dawn*, based on the supposed tragedy.

Another suggestion was that Port Quin men were drowned while attempting to molest another ship. It was also implied that fishermen fled when Customs officers arrived, having received word of their smuggling activities. This theory was aired when a Mrs D.M. Ellis visited Port Quin in 1898 and reported that the cottage windows were broken, with curtains blowing through them, and that the previous year the men had been trying to evade the Preventive Men. But the real cause was, no doubt, the mass emigration following the mine closure and the decline of the fishing industry.

Port Quin was again in the headlines in 1937 when *The People* newspaper splashed a headline about 'Britain's Loneliest Boy', and went on to report that Percy Dingle, aged eight years, was the only child among the twenty remaining adults in this small hamlet. Only during the school holidays in August did he have tourist playmates who like swallows departed, leaving him alone. The boy's nearest school was three and a half miles away at Tredrissick in the parish of St Minver, and each day he walked there and back.

At that time many of the old cottages were roofless and overgrown; there were no boats, nets or fishermen; no litter, no cafés; no bungaloid developments – and no happy children's voices.

The National Trust later bought several of the derelict cottages and attractively restored them so that they have become popular seasonal lettings. With the privately-owned fish cellars and a sprouting of more modern buildings including a restaurant above the inlet, Port Quin has emerged from its shrouded past. But among the restored cottages one can see vestiges of overgrown ruins that still hold their secrets, and up the valley in the Hop Garden where market gardening was carried on, traces of old cottagers' gardens can still be seen.

When we see Port Quin below us and its restored cottages sleeping in the sunshine, when the tide is high with scarcely a ripple for the swimmers, it is difficult to visualize the scene when a north-west winter gale screams into the inlet. Then gigantic waves sweep up over the rocks and break over the road with frightening power and it is then, while watching this spectacle, that one may think that perhaps there was, after all, some truth in those old legends.

WRECKS ON AND NEAR GREENAWAY

WHILE many ships started life in the Padstow boat-building yards, many ended their days on the Doom Bar, Greenaway Rocks, or at the bottom of Padstow Bay or Hayle Bay.

During February, 1818, three ships were wrecked and quantities of butter, lard, pork and beef were washed ashore when many parishioners from St Minver came out to reap the harvest. During their salvage attempts three men were drowned, leaving behind them twelve fatherless children.

In the following January, a vessel wrecked in the estuary provided a further opportunity for beachcombing by the locals. Some of the loot was secreted on the Commons, and on one occasion a party of 'bal maidens' (female surface-workers at a mine) clashed with another group of women who were also on the lookout. A box of figs was found and the women fought ferociously for two hours for this plunder. Some were almost stripped naked, but the bal maidens, no doubt made of sterner stuff, finally carried off the prize.

On the morning of February 6th, 1867 on an ebbing tide, the *Georgiana* of Boston, Lincolnshire was blown across the Doom Bar to the St Minver shore. All but one of the crew were rescued, but the Padstow lifeboat *Albert Edward* II which went to her assistance capsized and five of her crew were drowned. Next day the schooner was pounded to pieces.

In September 1875 the *Immacolata*, en route from Corfu, was wrecked off Greenaway. Her unusual cargo of bones was salvaged and placed at the end of a road at Greenaway and divided into lots of five to twenty tons for sale to manure merchants and others.

On April 11th, 1900 an even greater tragedy was witnessed from the cliffs of Greenaway, when the Lowestoft ketch *Peace and Plenty* got into difficulties in the bay. The oar-propelled Padstow lifeboat *Arab* went to her aid and, when nearly there, was overturned by a huge wave. Eight of the crew were washed overboard. The remainder managed to hold on and burned red flares to signal for help from Padstow's main lifeboat, the steam-driven *James Stevens No. 4*. Meanwhile, the *Peace and Plenty* had driven onto Greenaway rocks and three crewmen were drowned. Five others were saved by the rocket life-saving apparatus. The rocket apparatus was housed where Mr Tellam Hocking's shop now stands. The *Arab* had by now grounded and her crew, together with the eight washed overboard, were rescued. The *James Stevens No. 4*, heading towards the stricken *Arab*, was suddenly hit by another huge wave which turned her end-over-end and she too was dashed ashore, ending up in a cave without deck or engines. Eight of her crew drowned, and only three survived.

On November 12th, 1911 the *Arab No. 2* lifeboat was called to help the *Island Maid* and the *Angele*, both in difficulties at the same time. Six men were rescued from the *Island Maid* when she struck the Doom Bar. Then the *Arab* set sail again as the *Angele* struck, but the lifeboat crew, fatigued, could not reach her and a volunteer crew took over. They saved the *Angele*'s captain, but the crew were drowned. Later, four bodies were recovered and buried in St Enodoc churchyard.

In more modern times, on January 23rd, 1939 the ex-minelayer *Medea* was being towed from Portsmouth to a breaker's yard at Newport, Gwent, when she broke her tow-rope in an eighty-mile per-hour gale off Trevose Head,

33.   The wreck of the *Medea*

drifted into the mouth of the estuary and grounded on Greenaway rocks.

During the night, as searchlights from Trebetherick and Port Isaac coastguard teams lit up the scene, the crew were seen to be huddled together on the bridge, under constant battering by the heavy seas. The life-saving team fired six rockets with lines towards the *Medea*, which was separated from the shore by fifty yards of churning surf and jagged rocks. Five rockets missed their target, but the sixth and final one was successful and the crew of four were taken off by breeches buoy. A fifth member of the crew had been previously lost overboard.

FIELD NAMES

FIELD names are fascinating and St Minver parish has its share of unusual ones, which I have culled from old Rate records, etc.

Gallows Hill Field presents intriguing questions: what happened to the gallows; who was hung from it; are there skeletons rattling in local cupboards?

What was the significance of Frying Pan Field?

Who was the weaver who lived at Weaver's Bottom?

Was Lightening Purse Meadow a habitat for petty thieving?

Who was the Grandfather who owned the meadow of that name?

Who was the Lady who owned Madame's Orchard?

Was the soil of Hornywink (=lapwing) as poor and desolate as its Cornish dialect implies or was the field the habitat of this bird?

Was Mean Ground equally as bad?

More straightforward are the names given by the owners or occupiers of Blake's Meadow, Cater's Moor, Dalley's Tenement, Slogget's Meadow and Tristram's Bed, but I am still trying to find the association of Box Heater Field with the old-fashioned iron (box heater) box with a red hot iron inside; or is there a plant of this name?

FEASTS AND FESTIVITIES IN ST MINVER PARISH

St James's tide around July 25th was a time of celebration for the parishioners of St Minver and neighbouring St Kew. The first three days were devoted to various amusements and hospitality at home. On the fourth day (the Wednesday) many people went to Polzeath to 'wash away St James', and the day became known as St James' Wednesday. In the licences granted by the Excise it was named St Minver Feast, and during the 1867 celebrations an estimated 2,000 people took part, arriving on foot, horseback, and in some hundred wagons and carts. The Feast Day of St Minver's St Menefreda is on November 24th.

In days gone by much was made of national events and St Minver parish was never behind when it came to staging a celebration. On the Silver Jubilee of King George V and Queen Mary on May 6th, 1935 a large assembly met at the cricket field, where a united service was held at 2 p.m. followed by the presentation of a flagstaff and a Union Jack flag which was then hoisted. St Minver Silver Band played continuously, during which time the adults' and childrens' sports got under way with such highlights as ladies' and gents' tug-of-war, sack and three-legged races, high jump, obstacle and wheelbarrow races. Children were regaled with a free tea and a Jubilee mug. Prizes were distributed at 7.45 p.m. followed by the ascent of fire balloons. As dusk descended there was a firework display with exotically-named set pieces in the programme: 'Special Chinese Device with Roman Candles, Parachute Rockets and Jack-in-the-Box, a Vertical Wheel Device with Queen Mary Rockets, Mine of Serpents and *Feu de Joie*, followed by The Prince of Wales Feathers Device and ending with The Brilliant Sun'. At 10 p.m. a whist drive started at the St Minver Institute, and at the Rock Institute the Bugle Bohemian Orchestra played music to a happy crowd of dancers until 2 a.m., making the twelve-hour non-stop celebrations a huge success.

Two years later St Minver was celebrating the Coronation of George VI and Queen Elizabeth, with an almost identical timetable of events, though the dance ended one hour earlier.

A curious custom was once held annually on November 4th when boys assembled in the church porch carrying empty turnip lanterns. Here they were met by the churchwardens who presented each of them with a candle which was then placed into the lantern and lighted. The boys then paraded through the village swinging their lanterns which they finally dashed to pieces against a convenient wall and sometimes against the door of some unpopular person. On the same evening the churchwardens entertained the bell ringers to supper at the village inn.

The Parish Registers show that St Minver people were a caring community, for it is recorded that on October 10th, 1666 there was 'collected in this parish for the supply of the citizens of London whose great loss was occasioned by that dreadful fire which burnt the greatest part of the city, the sum of one pound and one penny'.

Not all St Minver folk were so beneficent. Samuel Symons and Henry Symons, together with Thomas Kendall, stole two bullocks from William Blake and were convicted and sentenced to transportation for life.

J. BOSANKOE

LONG before the late Poet Laureate Sir John Betjeman immortalized the St Minver area in his glowing prose and poetry, the parish had its own poet, a worthy named J.Bosankoe, who died in 1907 aged seventy-seven years.

Bosankoe produced a considerable amount of verse about local people, organizations, events, places, and the seasons. Much of the verses was doggerel and similar to the outpourings of the dreadful nineteenth-century Scottish post William McGonagall.

Of St Minver Lowlands Parish Council he wrote:

> Now all the Councillors will have
> To come like poor men to the grave,
> And if their stewardship be right
> They need not fear the Master's sight.
> The Parish Council went off well
> The twelve men chosen I can tell,
> The chairman there that took the lead
> Done what was right by word and deed.

He gives ominous warnings to the parish Band of Hope:

St Minver Band of Hope is here
And many of the children dear
Will leave alone the gin and beer.
From all intoxicants steer clear.
The drink, young ladies all should dread
And never with a drunkard wed.
For many wives and children dear
Have suffered in the past, I fear.

He sees the future development of Polzeath and would no doubt, if he were alive today, write more strongly on the inflated prices of land.

A lovely place is Polseath beach
Unto Pentire cliff it reach.
As I have been told by someone about
It is a mile when tide is out . . .
And then I see another move
And Polseath may still now improve
Six houses to be built, I hear.
The land is bought, but rather dear.

The seasons flow from his pen as he compares them with the life span of Man:

We see the dewdrop in the morn
That sparkles like the growing corn,
And there the hedges decked so gay
With flowers in the month of May.
The harvest comes – a waiting time
To gather in Earth's fruits, we find
And now there is a-plenty here
For man and beast all hearts to cheer.
The leaves are fading on the tree
Showing us what man must be,

The autumn shown upon him here
Like falling leaves – he'll disappear.

Mr Bosankoe was one of a number of Cornish village poets,
amongst whom the West Cornwall miner John Harris (1820-
1884) stood head and shoulders above the rest.

There is little comparison between Bosankoe's Seasons poem
and the haunting lyrical effect of Harris's blank verse on the
same subject:

> Summer was past, and in the lifeless wood
> Autumn lay down to die.
> Deep mourning tones
> Arose from Nature, and the sky wept tears
> Upon the sounding earth.

Later, the parish of St Minver was to provide inspiration
for John Betjeman, one of the most celebrated poets of the
twentieth century:

> The tide is high and a sleepy Atlantic sends
> Exploring ripple on ripple down Polzeath shore,
> And the gathering dark is full of the thought of friends
> I shall see no more . . .
> What a host of stars in a wideness still and deep:
> What a host of souls, as a motorbike whines away
> And the silver snake of the estuary curls to sleep
> In Daymer Bay.

BIBLIOGRAPHY AND FURTHER READING

Life in Cornwall in the Nineteenth Century. Vols 1, 2, 3, 4. Bradford
Barton, Truro. 1970–1974

Companion Guide to Devon and Cornwall. D. Bates. William Collins &
Co. Ltd, London. 1976

An Introduction to Cornish Water Mills. D. E. Benny. Bradford Barton

The Nature of Cornwall. Rene Bere. Barracuda Books Ltd, Buckingham

Portrait of Cornwall. Claude Berry. Robert Hale, Ltd, Clerkenwall
Green, London, E.C.1. 1963

Betjeman's Cornwall. John Betjeman. John Murray (Publishers) Ltd, 50
Albemarle Street, London W1X 4BD

Flowers of the Countryside. M. and P. Blamey. William Collins & Co.
Ltd, London. 1980

What to look for in Cornish Churches. H. Miles Brown. David & Charles,
Newton Abbot, Devon. 1973

The Naturalist in Devon and Cornwall. R. Burrows. David & Charles Ltd.
1971

Survey of Cornwall. Richard Carew. 1602

Cornish Shipwrecks. The North Cornish Coast. Vol. 2. Clive Carter. David
& Charles. 1970

Cornish Feasts and Folklore. M. A. Courtenay

Cornish Windmills. H. L. Douch. Oscar Blackford, Ltd, Truro

Old Cornish Inns. H. L. Douch. Bradford Barton

The River Camel. B. Duxberry & M. Williams. Bossiney Books, St Teath, Bodmin. 1987

Cornish Church Guide. Charles Henderson. Oscar Blackford. 1928

A Book About Smuggling in the West Country. Antony D. Hippisley-Coxe. Tabb House, Padstow. 1984

Kelly's Directories. Various. Kelly's Directories, Ltd, 186 Strand, London, W.C.2

A Complete Parochial Parish History of the County of Cornwall, Vol.III. 1870. William Lake, Boscawan Street, Truro

Holy Wells of Cornwall. The Rev. A.J. Lane-Davies, Federation of Old Cornwall Societies. 1970

Parochial and Family History of the Deanery of Trigg Minor. Sir John Maclean. 1868

The King's England. Cornwall. Arthur Mee. Hodder & Stoughton Ltd, London, E.C.4. 1967

Murray's Handbook of Devon and Cornwall. John Murray. 1851

Ports and Harbours of Cornwall. Richard Pearse. Warne, St Austell. 1963

Cornish Villages. Donald R. Rawe. Robert Hale Ltd. 1978

The National Trust in Cornwall. Aerial Views of Property on the North Cornish Coast. Skyshots, St Ives, Cornwall

A Short History of the Churches and Parish of St Minver, Cornwall. The Rev. Harold A. Thomas, Oscar Blackford. 1929

The Stone Peninsula. James Turner. William Kimber Ltd, 22a Queen Anne's Gate, London, SW1 9AE. 1975

The Story of Port Isaac, Port Gaverne and Port Quin. Monica Winstanley. Lodenek Press Ltd, Padstow. 1973

An Introduction to the Archaeology of Cornwall. Charles Woolf. Bradford Barton. 1970